KING ARTHUR AND HIS KNIGHTS

King Arthur and His Knights

Adapted by William Kottmeyer
St. Louis Public Schools

Illustrated by MURRAY McKEEHAN

Phoenix Learning Resources
New York

The Phoenix Everyreaders

The EVERYREADERS were selected from the great literature of the world and adapted to the needs of today's children. This series retains the flavor of the originals, providing mature content and dramatic plot structure, along with eye appeal designed to motivate reading.

This approach was first developed in the renowned St. Louis Reading Clinic by Dr. Kottmeyer and is the direct outgrowth of wide and successful teaching of remedial reading.

A high interest level plus the carefully controlled vocabulary and sentence structure enable pupils to read the stories easily, confidently, and with enjoyment.

Copyright © 1988, 1952 by Phoenix Learning Resources, Inc. All Rights Reserved. No part of this publication may be reproduced, stored in a retrieval system, or transmitted, in any form or by any means, electronic, mechanical, photocopying, recording, or otherwise, without the prior written permission of the publisher. Printed in the United States of America.

ISBN 0-7915-1367-X
(Previously ISBN 0-07-033732-2)

Contents

Arthur Becomes King...................... 1

The Wonderful Sword Excalibur............ 13

The Round Table Comes to Camelot.......... 29

The Story of False Vivien and Merlin......... 35

The Evil Plan of Morgan le Fay.............. 43

The Kitchen Knight...................... 61

Sir Galahad and the Holy Grail........ 83

Sir Lancelot Saves the Queen............... 97

Death of King Arthur......................111

Arthur Becomes King

Many years ago Uther fought to make himself King of all England. Two true friends helped him. One was wise Merlin, the famous magician. The other was a great knight and fighter named Ulfius. At last Uther beat his enemies and became king.

Then Uther married Igraine, a widow. She had three daughters, Elaine, Margaret, and Morgan le Fay. Morgan le Fay could do more magic than anyone but Merlin. The girls soon married three kings who had made friends with Uther.

Soon after, Uther and Igraine had a son. Merlin went to Uther.

"King, you know that sometimes I can tell what will happen ahead of time. Listen to what is coming. You will die soon. Your enemies will rise again. They will want to kill your son so he will not become king. I beg you to do as I say. Let Sir Ulfius and me take him away and hide him. When he grows up we will bring him back to be king."

"Merlin," said Uther, "you are a wise man. We all have to die. If I must die soon, you had better hide the boy. My enemies do not yet know I have a son."

So Merlin and Ulfius hid the boy. Only they knew where he was. A little later Uther got sick and died.

Everything happened as Merlin had said. Uther's enemies rose and fought one another. Robbers and killers went free in the land. No man was strong enough to rule. The years passed. At last the chief bishop of the church sent for Merlin.

"Merlin," he said, "men tell me you are wiser than all other men. Can you not save our land from war and killing? Choose a strong leader. He will be the king over us."

"My lord," said Merlin, "sometimes I can tell what will happen before it does. Soon our land will have such a king. He will be wiser and greater than Uther. I tell you too that he shall be Uther's true son."

"You tell me wonderful news, Merlin," said the Bishop. "When will he come? How shall we know him?"

"Say no more," said Merlin. "I shall find a way so all will know him. Call all the lords and great knights to London for Christmas. Have them all come to the great church there."

The Bishop did as Merlin had said. As they came to London, all saw a strange thing. Before the great church was a square block of stone. On it was an iron anvil. A wonderful steel sword was stuck in the anvil. The handle was gold, with shining jewels. On the stone were these words —
>   He who can pull out this sword
>   is the King of England.

A great crowd of knights and lords came to London for Christmas. There would be a contest for the knights, and then they were to try to pull out the sword.

Among those who came to London was a good knight known as Sir Ector. Sir Ector had two sons. The older was Sir Kay, already known as a brave young knight. The other was a lad named Arthur. He carried Sir Kay's spear and shield but was not yet a knight. Sir Ector and his sons set up their tent with others near the contest field. Sir Kay was to fight in the contest.

The contest was to be a battle between two teams of knights. On the day of the battle the two teams began to fill their places. When all were ready a horn was blown. Each team raced its horses forward. They met with a crash like thunder. Horses fell and men were thrown. Spears broke into pieces. The men fought on with their swords.

Sir Kay threw two knights quickly before his horse went down. He fought on with his sword and brought down more. Then, fighting hard with another knight, he hit him squarely on his steel helmet. The knight fell, but Sir Kay's sword snapped in two. He fought his way clear to the wall. Arthur, watching his brother, ran to him.

"Brother," cried Sir Kay, "get me another sword. Hurry to the tent. Our men have some there."

Arthur ran back to the tent. But no one was there. All had gone to watch the battle. Not a sword could Arthur find.

Then he remembered seeing the sword in the anvil near the church. He ran quickly to the church, which was nearby. No one was guarding the sword. Without seeing the words, Arthur jumped on the stone. He put his hand on the sword and easily pulled it out.

Back on the field, Sir Kay was waiting. He saw Arthur come running.

"Do you have it?" he called.

"Here," said Arthur, handing him the sword.

Sir Kay knew the sword as soon as he saw it.

"Where did you get this sword?" he cried.

"Why," said Arthur, "I could find none in the tent. I pulled this one out of the anvil before the church. What's the matter?"

"Nothing," said Sir Kay. "Run and find our father. Tell him to come quickly to our tent."

When Sir Ector came to the tent he saw Sir Kay's face was white.

"What is the matter, my son?" he cried.

"Look!" said Sir Kay. He pointed to the sword.

Sir Ector's mouth fell open. He knew the sword well.

"Where did you get it?" he cried.

Sir Kay smiled. "I've got it. What's the difference?"

"If you pulled it out, you are to be King of England," said Sir Ector. "But if you pulled it out, you can put it back again. It is not yet the time to do it."

Sir Kay began to be afraid. But he thought that if Arthur was able to pull out the sword, surely he could do it, too.

"Come," said Sir Ector. The two started off for the great church. Arthur followed. When they came to the anvil, they found it smooth. Sir Kay pushed and pushed at the sword. He could not even scratch the anvil.

"How did you pull it out?" asked Sir Ector.

"Let me put it back," said Arthur, coming forward.

"You? What right have you to touch it, boy?"

"Why, I pulled it out," said Arthur.

Sir Ector looked at him strangely. Then he looked at Kay. "Try it," he said at last.

Arthur took the sword and jumped upon the stone. He pushed the sword easily deep into the iron. Then he pulled it out again and pushed it back.

Sir Ector rubbed his eyes. "I can't believe it!" he cried.

Then he fell on his knees before Arthur.

"Father!" cried Arthur. "Why do you kneel before me?"

"Boy," said Sir Ector, "I am not your father. You must be a king's son or you could not have pulled out the sword."

"What?" cried Arthur unhappily. "Father, please do not kneel before me. Tell me what you mean!"

"Listen, then," said Sir Ector. "Years ago the wise magician, Merlin, came to me. He told me to be at King Uther's castle gate at midnight. That night I did as he said. Merlin and Sir Ulfius, Uther's best friends, came. Merlin carried a baby in his arms. That baby was you, Arthur."

"Merlin told me to bring you up as my own son. He said no one must know who you were. I told Merlin I would do as he said. I never knew who your father was. Now I can guess. You must be King Uther's son. Who else could have pulled out the sword?"

"I would rather be your son than be a king!" cried Arthur.

"Come," said Sir Ector. "On Christmas the Bishop will give everyone a chance to pull the sword. You must take your turn."

On Christmas Day the great crowd of knights and lords and kings gathered before the church. The Bishop had a horn blown to start the trial.

First came the kings who had once joined with King Uther. King Lot, husband of Queen Igraine's daughter Margaret, stepped forward. He took hold of the sword with both hands and pulled with all his might. Again and again he tried. The sword did not move. Angrily King Lot stepped back.

Now came the others, kings, lords, and knights. They pulled and pushed, but not one could make the sword move.

"What trick of Merlin's is this?" they cried. "No man can move this sword. Come, choose one of us to be king."

The Bishop held up his hand. "Let no man speak against the wisest of us all. There comes Merlin. He will speak for himself."

All turned to look. Down the street came Merlin and Sir Ulfius. Behind them came Sir Ector with Sir Kay and Arthur.

Merlin led them to where the sword was.

"Who are these men?" asked the Bishop.

"Here is one who will try the sword," said Merlin. He laid his hand on Arthur's shoulder. "Here, lords of England, is the true son of King Uther!"

"But Uther had no son!" cried the Bishop.

And so Merlin told the story again. Sir Ulfius said, "Here am I to say Merlin speaks true."

"Then let him try," said the Bishop.

Arthur stepped upon the stone. He laid his hand on the sword. Smoothly and easily he pulled it out. He held it high so all could see.

The lords and knights did not know what to say or do. Some were ready to have Arthur. Others would not. "A boy to be our king?" they cried. "No! This is a trick of Merlin and Sir Ulfius!"

But others began to shout for Arthur. "Arthur, King of England! Arthur, King of England."

To make sure that all was fair, the Bishop had other trials in other places. Each time only Arthur pulled the sword free. Each time he won more friends. At last the Bishop put the crown upon his head.

So Arthur became King of all England. Some of the kings and lords did not want him, and he had to fight them. As the years went by, he became stronger and greater. Knights came from all lands to be in his court. At Camelot Arthur started the famous Knights of the Round Table. These were the greatest of all the knights. They made their names famous for all time. All who love the old stories will remember Sir Lancelot of the Lake, Sir Galahad, who found the Holy Grail, Sir Gawain, and Sir Gareth.

The Wonderful Sword Excalibur

Not long after Arthur became king, he and his friends were resting in a castle. They had been going from city to city meeting the people. A knight came riding slowly to the castle. A boy walked beside him holding him up on his horse. His shield and armor were red with blood. A great wound in his side still bled as he rode.

"Give help to that poor knight," cried King Arthur. "Sir Kay, bring the boy to us. Let us hear what has happened."

They brought the wounded knight to King Arthur's doctor. The boy came before the King.

"Who is your master?" asked King Arthur. "How was he so badly hurt?"

"My lord," said the boy, "he is Sir Miles. He set out to find adventures as a good knight should. This morning we came to a castle deep in the forest. Before the castle lay a broad flat field. We crossed a stone bridge. On one side stood a tree. Many shields hung in this tree. On the bridge was a big black shield. Near it hung a great hammer. Under the shield were the words —

> He who strikes this shield
> risks his life.

"Sir Miles took the hammer and hit the shield. It rang out like thunder. The great gate of the castle was lowered. Out rode a mighty knight in black armor. His horse, his shield — everything was black.

"'So,' he cried, 'you struck the shield! Now I will take your shield away. I shall hang it on the tree with the others.'

"'If you can,' said Sir Miles.

"Then the two knights charged. They met near the middle of the field. Sir Miles' spear broke into splinters. The Black Knight's spear drove through my master's shield and into his side. He fell from his horse and lay on the ground.

"Then the Black Knight took my master's shield and hung it with the others. He rode off to the castle. The gate lowered again to let him in and closed. I got my master on his horse and came here."

King Arthur was very angry. "This is no true knight," he cried. "He leaves a wounded knight on the field. He takes his shield when he has fought fair. I will go myself to teach this Black Knight a lesson."

King Arthur's knights begged him to send one of them. He would not do so. "I go myself," he said, "and I go alone."

The next morning King Arthur set out. He rode into the forest the way the boy told him to go. On the way he saw a strange sight. Three men were chasing an old white-haired man. A big fellow with a knife in his hand was about to catch him.

"Here is work to do for a good knight,"

said King Arthur. He turned his horse aside and rode swiftly after the men. When the three saw him coming, they turned and ran. The old man stopped. King Arthur caught the old man's horse and rode to him.

"What?" he cried. "Merlin! What are you doing here? I just left you at the castle! It's a good thing that I came by."

The wise old Merlin smiled. "They could not have hurt me," he said. "I was in no danger. But you, my lord, will soon be in great danger. That is why I am here. Let me go with you. You will need me."

"You may come, Merlin," said Arthur, "but do not try to keep me from this adventure. I am not afraid."

So Merlin and King Arthur rode on in the forest. Before long, they came to the bridge the boy had told them of. There, too, they saw the tree full of shields. Farther on lay the broad field and the castle.

"Look, Merlin!" cried Arthur. "This Black Knight must be a mighty fighter. See how many shields hang in the tree."

"You, my lord, will be very lucky if your shield does not hang there today," said Merlin.

"I will fight him anyway," said Arthur. He rode forward to the bridge. There, as the boy had said, hung the black shield and hammer. King Arthur struck the shield a mighty blow.

The sound had hardly died when the castle gate dropped. Out rode the Black Knight.

"Did you read the words?" he cried. "Now I shall take your shield from you. Or will you give it up?"

"I came here to fight you," said Arthur. "Say no more. Get ready."

King Arthur now rode to one side of the field. The Black Knight rode to the other. Then both dug their spurs into their horses. The horses sprang forward. They crashed together. Both spears broke into splinters. Had the two men not been great riders they would have fallen. King Arthur was much surprised that the Black Knight had not gone down. They turned and met again in the middle of the field.

"I do not know you," said Arthur, "but you are a strong knight. Get down and we will fight on foot with swords."

"Not yet," said the Black Knight. "Let us try again. Here are new spears."

Two boys now rode from the castle. Each carried a strong new spear. The Black Knight took one; King Arthur took the other. Again they rode away from each other and turned. Again they charged.

King Arthur's spear struck the Black Knight's shield hard and square. Again it flew into pieces. But this time the Black Knight's spear did not break. Straight through Arthur's shield it went. The King's saddle broke loose. Only his great skill saved him. He jumped clear and landed on his feet. Before the Black Knight could move, Arthur forced his horse back. To save himself the Black Knight slid to the ground.

Now each pulled loose his sword and ran at the other. They hacked mighty blows at each other. Bits of armor began to fly. Now and then a sword bit deep. Both began to drip blood.

At last Arthur struck a mighty blow. It landed with a crash on the Black Knight's helmet. He cried out in pain and went to his knees. The King could have won, then, for the Black Knight was helpless. But Arthur held only the sword handle of his sword! The mighty blow had broken the sword into pieces.

The Black Knight looked up. He threw aside his shield. He took his own sword with both hands and swung. The blow broke through Arthur's shield and helmet. The blood and sweat rolled into the King's eyes. He sank to his knees, blinded.

"Give up your shield!" cried the Black Knight.

"Never!" cried Arthur. He reached out and caught the other by the belt. He pulled himself to his feet. He pushed his leg behind the Black Knight's legs and threw him backward. The Black Knight lay as if he were dead.

King Arthur now fell forward upon him.

He pulled the laces loose and tore off the helmet.

"King Pellinore!" he cried.

The Black Knight was King Pellinore, a strong king who had fought King Arthur. Arthur's men had driven him into the forests but had never caught him.

Pellinore now opened his eyes. He saw the blood run from Arthur's head and knew he must be weak. Suddenly he caught the King's arm and rolled over upon him. Now he pulled Arthur's helmet loose and reached for his dagger.

As he raised his arm for the last blow something came crashing down on his head. Everything went black before his eyes. He rolled over senseless. Merlin, who had come quietly up to them, threw aside the Black Knight's sword.

"You have killed him," cried King Arthur.

"Oh, no," said Merlin calmly. "He will wake up in an hour or two. But if we don't care for you, you will die."

Arthur crawled weakly to his knees.

Merlin helped him on his horse. Together they rode into the forest.

"I know an old man near here," said Merlin. "He can care for your wound."

There Merlin took the King. The two old men laid him on a bed. They washed his wound and cared for it. Arthur was too weak to raise his head.

While King Arthur lay in the old man's hut, a crowd of lords and ladies came by. With them was the beautiful Lady Guinevere. When Guinevere saw the King's war horse outside the hut, she asked whose it was. Merlin took her inside. She thought she had never seen a finer knight than the wounded Arthur. Merlin did not tell her who he was.

"I have a wise doctor at my castle," she said. "He has a wonderful medicine for wounds. I shall send him. He will cure this knight."

King Arthur thought Guinevere the most beautiful woman in the world. So Arthur first met the lady who was to become his queen.

Guinevere's doctor came the next day. So wonderful was the medicine that Arthur's wound was quickly healed.

"Merlin," said Arthur, "I must go again to fight Pellinore. He is the strongest and best fighter I have ever met. If I had not broken my sword, I should have won."

"My lord," said Merlin, "you are lucky to be alive. You have no sword or spear. How can you fight without them?"

"I know not. But I will fight him again."

"All right. I will not try to stop you. I will help you. Listen to me. There is in this forest a magic lake. Sometimes men have seen a wonderful thing there. A woman's arm comes out of the water. In her hand she holds a sword. It is a strange and wonderful sword. The name of this sword is Excalibur. Many knights have tried to get it. When they come near, the arm goes back under the water. I will take you to the lake. If you can get the sword, you can fight anyone."

"Take me to the lake," said Arthur.

Merlin again led the way back into the

forest. At last they came to the banks of the lake. Merlin pointed to the middle of the lake. A woman's white arm reached out of the water. In her hand was the beautiful sword, as Merlin had said.

As they looked, a woman came walking toward them.

"Good day, King Arthur," she said. "What brings you here?"

"How do you know me?" asked Arthur. "Who are you?"

"I am the Lady of the Lake. I know many things. I am glad to see you, but why have you come?"

"I fought a knight and broke my sword in the battle. Merlin told me of Excalibur. I am here to get it if I can."

"That is not easy. Many have tried and failed. The man who gets Excalibur must do no wrong and have no fear."

"That is sad news," said Arthur. "I fear no man, but I cannot say I do no wrong. I would like to try. Will you tell me how?"

"I will do what I can to help you," said the Lady of the Lake.

As she spoke a little boat came up to the shore. She pointed to it. King Arthur stepped in. The boat turned itself and moved out on the lake. Straight to the sword it went.

King Arthur reached out and took the sword. The arm went down. Arthur held the sword and the cover in his hand.

Arthur looked at the sword happily. It was more beautiful than he had dreamed. The boat turned again and moved to the shore. Merlin and the Lady of the Lake were waiting.

"Lady," cried King Arthur, "I thank you with all my heart. Now I have the most wonderful sword in the world."

"You shall make it the most famous," said the Lady.

King Arthur and Merlin now made their way back through the forest. About noon the next day they came again to Pellinore's castle. Arthur rode straight to the black shield. He smashed the hammer against it. As before, King Pellinore came riding from the castle.

"King Pellinore," said Arthur, "let us waste no time in words. Are you ready?"

King Pellinore turned and rode to his side of the field. Again the two boys rode out with a spear for each. The two kings called to their horses and drove forward. Both spears broke into pieces.

Pellinore and King Arthur jumped lightly from their horses. Each pulled out his sword. Their blows fell like thunder upon shield and armor. But now the battle went differently. Soon Excalibur began to bite through Pellinore's armor. Arthur did not get a scratch. Then a mighty blow drove Pellinore to his knees.

"Give me my life!" he cried. "I give up to you."

"I will," said Arthur. "And I will give you back your lands if you call me your king."

And so King Pellinore became Sir Pellinore. He became Arthur's good friend. He and his sons later became famous knights of the Round Table.

Merlin and King Arthur rode back next

day to their friends. As they rode, Merlin spoke to King Arthur.

"My lord, which would you rather have — Excalibur or the sword cover?"

Arthur laughed. "Excalibur," he said.

"You are wrong," said Merlin. "Excalibur is a wonderful sword. But he who has Excalibur's cover will never be wounded. Do you not remember? When you fought Pellinore you were not hurt. That was because you had the cover. Keep both the sword and the cover."

"Merlin, I shall use Excalibur to fight only when I need it."

He built a strong box. Here he kept both sword and cover tightly locked. Only when enemies fought his people did King Arthur take Excalibur to battle. He kept Excalibur until he died, as you shall read. The cover was later stolen from him. That gave him much pain, as you shall also hear.

The Round Table Comes to Camelot

After King Arthur got the sword Excalibur, he thought often of the beautiful Lady Guinevere.

"We should have a queen," he said to Merlin. "I will marry no other lady but the Lady Guinevere."

Old Merlin shook his head. "She will bring you much trouble," he said.

"I will have her and no other," said King Arthur. "Go to her father and speak for me."

Merlin did as King Arthur told him. The Lady Guinevere was willing. Her father was glad King Arthur had chosen his daughter. And so Guinevere, her ladies, and her father came to Camelot. At dinner Guinevere's father spoke to King Arthur.

"What shall I give you as a present?" he asked. "It is hard to find something a king does not have. Tell me what it shall be."

King Arthur laughed. "Merlin," he said, "what shall I ask?"

Merlin said, "My lord, long ago I had a table made for King Uther. It was like a ring, so men called it the Round Table. It had seats for 150 men. These men were to be the greatest knights in the world. When a knight won a seat, his name went on the chair in gold letters.

"The center seat was for the king. Straight across was the Seat of Danger. No name ever showed on this seat. It was for the greatest knight who would ever live. If anyone else sat here, he was to die. All the seats were never filled in King Uther's time. When King Uther died, he left the Round Table to Guinevere's father. He has no band of brave knights. No one uses the Round Table.

"Now I say that he should give you the

Round Table. While you are king you shall fill every seat. Even the Seat of Danger shall be filled."

"That would be a wonderful present," cried King Arthur.

"You shall have it, then," said Guinevere's father.

The Round Table was brought to Camelot. After the wedding of King Arthur and Guinevere, the table was set up.

At each place was a gold cup and a gold plate. Merlin took Arthur's hand and led him to his seat. The gold letters spelled

Arthur, King.

Merlin pointed to the Seat of Danger.

"Only one man may sit there," he said. "That man is not yet born. If anyone else dares sit there, he will die."

"Merlin," cried King Arthur. "Choose the knights to fill the table."

"Do not hurry, my lord," said Merlin. "You will become greater as more seats are taken. When the seats are taken you can become no greater. That will be the end for you."

"Then choose as many as you can."

"A knight must earn his seat at the Round Table," said Merlin. "Some have. Them I shall choose."

Merlin looked around the hall. First he saw Sir Pellinore.

"Here is a great knight," he said. "Next to you he is the best fighter."

He took Sir Pellinore by the hand. He led him to the seat at King Arthur's left. Suddenly gold letters were seen on the chair — Pellinore.

Merlin then chose other knights and led them to their seats. Sir Ulfius won a seat. Sir Kay, King Arthur's brother, had another. Sir Gawain, son of King Lot and Arthur's sister, was also chosen. Many other brave and famous knights were chosen that day.

"Why is the seat at my right empty?" asked King Arthur.

"That is for the greatest fighter you shall have," said Merlin. "He shall be greatest until the one comes to sit in the Seat of Danger."

Then each knight rose and held up his sword handle. They all agreed as to what they would do.

"I will be kind to the weak.
I will be brave against the strong.
I will fight all who do wrong.
I will fight for those who cannot fight.
I will help those who call me for help.
I will harm no woman.
I will help my brother knights.
I will be true to my friends.
I will be faithful in love."

When they had said these words, each knight swore to do these things. In later years some knights died or were killed. Then their names would go off the chairs. When a knight had proved himself, he might become a knight of the Round Table. Knights and lords came to Camelot to join Arthur's men. So brave were the Knights of the Round Table that they became famous over the whole world.

The Story of False Vivien and Merlin

Not long after the Round Table was started, King Arthur lost some knights in war. He and Merlin chose others to fill their places. All the places were filled but the Seat of Danger and one other.

Now there were two young knights who had fought bravely. One was Sir Tor. He was Sir Pellinore's son. The other was a son of Queen Morgan le Fay. At last King Arthur chose Sir Tor for a seat at the Round Table.

When Queen Morgan le Fay heard this she was angry. "So!" she cried, "I am King Arthur's sister, but he does not care. He will not choose my son. He would rather have this Sir Tor. I will pay him for this."

She went to King Arthur and told him she was going to leave.

"Sister," said King Arthur, "I am sorry you are angry. I would rather have taken your son than Sir Tor. But I think Sir Tor had more right to the seat. I must do what is right."

"I do not want to be near you any longer," she said. "I will leave your court."

"Lady," said King Arthur, "you may do what you wish."

Queen Morgan le Fay became King Arthur's enemy. She went to her own land to plan how she might get even with him. Morgan le Fay was a bad enemy to have. Next to Merlin she knew more magic than anyone else. Merlin himself had taught her much in the days of King Uther.

The more Queen Morgan thought about her son, the angrier she got. "I will not rest until King Arthur is dead," she said to herself. She knew that one man stood in her way — Merlin. Merlin was wiser than she, and Merlin would let no harm come to Arthur. "To kill Arthur," she said, "I must first get rid of Merlin."

Now in Morgan's castle lived a lovely girl named Vivien. Vivien was wise and clever for one so young. She was also cruel and cold. Queen Morgan liked her and had taught her what magic she knew. The girl had learned fast. Queen Morgan saw she could use Vivien to get Merlin.

"Vivien," she said one day, "I have taught you all I know. The greatest magician in the world is Merlin. There are many things he did not teach me. You must go to Merlin to learn more."

"I do not know him," said Vivien. "He will not want to give his secrets away to me."

Morgan smiled wisely. "Above all things Merlin loves beauty. You are the most beautiful girl in all the world. He will not be able to say no to you. Merlin has a great power he cannot give to anyone else. He can tell what will happen before it comes to pass. He can tell what will happen to others only. He cannot see what will happen to him. He told me this years ago.

"I want you to go to Merlin. When he sees you, he will not say no to what you ask. Also, I have here two magic rings. One has a white stone, the other red. The one who wears the red stone will love the one who wears the white. You will give the red stone to Merlin. You will keep the white one yourself. Then he will do as you say."

"But will he not be angry if he finds out I have tricked him?"

"Yes, he will. He may even use his magic against you. So, when he has taught you all he knows, you must get rid of him. If you do not, you will be in danger. Are you willing to try?"

"I would do anything to learn his magic."

Queen Morgan laughed. She gave Vivien the rings. Vivien thanked her and set out for King Arthur's castle.

Before long, the clever Vivien was able to get to Merlin. She knelt before him.

"What do you want?" asked Merlin crossly.

Vivien smiled. "I have a present for you," she said. She slipped the magic ring on Merlin's finger.

"Who gives me this ring?" he asked.

"The Queen Morgan le Fay," said Vivien.

"I hope this is no trick," said Merlin.

"No one could trick Merlin," said Vivien. "You are the wisest man in the world."

Merlin looked closer at lovely Vivien. As he looked the magic began to work. Vivien laughed and turned away. Merlin would not let her go. Before long, the knights and ladies all knew old Merlin loved the beautiful girl.

"Tell me what I can do for you," he said one day.

"Sir," said Vivien, "I want only one thing. I want to learn your magic. If you would teach me that, I would love you."

"That would be very foolish of me," said Merlin. He looked hard at the girl.

"Teach me, Merlin!" she cried. "Teach me and I will love you all my life."

At last Merlin agreed. "We will go to a castle I have in the forest," he said. So Vivien asked King Arthur if she might leave. Arthur let her go. The next day Merlin and Vivien set out for the lonely castle.

For more than a year Merlin and Vivien lived in the castle. At last Merlin said, "Vivien, I have taught you all I can. No one in all the world knows more magic than you."

"Only you," thought Vivien to herself. "I must get rid of you."

The next day Vivien had a fine dinner for Merlin. Then she brought in a cup of wine. She held it to Merlin's lips. Merlin drank. As soon as he had drunk it, he knew something was wrong. His eyes grew heavy. He tried to get to his feet, but fell back into his chair. He turned to look at Vivien. She was sitting quietly, smiling.

"Vivien," cried Merlin, "you have tricked me!" All went black before him.

Vivien laughed. "Merlin," she cried, "You are in my power! Poor fool, you cannot move. I will not let you go. Now I am the greatest magician in the world."

"This is my own fault," said Merlin. "I can blame only myself. Now, Vivien, do one last thing for me."

"What is it?"

"Soon King Arthur will be in great danger. Use your magic to save him. You can do this one last thing for me."

"All right," she said. "But you could not teach me to know what will happen. Where shall I find him?"

"Go to the castle of a knight called Sir Damas. When you get there, you will know what to do."

"I'll do it," said Vivien. "I guess I owe you one favor. And now — this is your end, Merlin."

She waved her hands over his body. Merlin lay as though he were dead. Then she called in some men.

"He is dead," she said. "Outside is a great stone box. Lay him inside. Then put the lid upon the box and cover him up."

The men found the box as Vivien had said. They laid Merlin inside. It took twenty men to lift the lid. Vivien then caused a thick cloud to form around the box. She sent everyone away from the castle. She herself now got ready to find the castle of Sir Damas.

And so ends the story of King Arthur's true friend, Merlin, the great magician. It was a sad day for King Arthur. He could have used Merlin often, as you shall soon see.

The Evil Plan of Morgan le Fay

Some time after Merlin and Vivien left Camelot, Queen Morgan came back.

"Brother," she said, "I am sorry I was angry with you. I have thought it over and I know you were right. I hope you will forgive me."

"Sister," said the kind King Arthur, "say no more. I am glad to have you back."

Queen Morgan knew what had happened to Merlin. Merlin was out of her way so she could put her plans to work.

"Brother," she said, "I have never seen your wonderful sword Excalibur. I have heard much about it. Could I not see it sometime?"

"I will show it to you now," said Arthur.

He took her to a room which she had never seen. Here Arthur opened a heavy locked box. Inside was Excalibur in the magic cover. Arthur handed it to Queen Morgan.

"It is the most beautiful sword I have ever seen," she cried. "Could I keep it a few days? I want to look at it again and again."

King Arthur did not want to make her angry again, so he said, "Take it."

The sly Queen took it to her room. Then she sent for gold and iron workers.

"Take this sword," she said. "Make me one just like it. Say nothing to anybody. I want to surprise our good king."

The men took the sword and went to work. After a few days they came back. They brought a sword which looked just like Excalibur. The Queen hid the two swords.

Not long after this, King Arthur and his friends went hunting. They soon saw a

deer and set out after it. The deer was fast and turned into the thick forest. Soon it had left all the hunters behind but two. These were King Arthur and a knight of the Round Table, Sir Accalon. Mile after mile they went. At last King Arthur shot the deer. He and Sir Accalon turned to go back. Before long, they knew they were lost.

They found a path through the trees and followed it. Just as night was coming on they came to a large lake. They went down to the shore. No one was in sight. As King Arthur looked out over the lake, he saw a boat. It came sailing fast to where they stood. It bumped softly on the sand near them. They saw no one on board.

"Let us look at this strange ship," said King Arthur.

"Go and I will follow," said Sir Accalon.

The two now stepped onto the boat. As they did several beautiful girls stepped out to meet them.

"Welcome, King Arthur. Welcome, Sir Accalon," they said.

"Fair ladies," said King Arthur, "who are you? How do you know us?"

"We know you were hunting and are hungry and tired. We came to meet you. Come, sit down, for we have food and drink for you."

So King Arthur and Sir Accalon went on board. The women led them to a room where a table was set. Here they asked King Arthur to sit down. They led Sir Accalon to another room where they also had set a table. The two tired men sat down and began to eat and drink. Soon King Arthur could hardly keep his eyes open.

"Have you a place to sleep?" he asked.

Soon the King was sound asleep. He never knew how long he slept, but at last he awoke. At first he thought he must be dreaming. Looking around him, he saw he lay in a long dark room. He could see iron bars across a small window. Sitting up now, he saw there were many other men in the room.

"Sir," he said to one nearby, "where are we? And who are you?"

"Sir," said the man, "you are locked in the castle of Sir Damas. All of us are his prisoners."

"How did I get here?"

"Some men carried you in last night. You were sound asleep."

"But who is this Sir Damas?" asked Arthur.

"He is not a true knight, but a coward. He has great power here, though, and is rich. There are two brothers. One is Sir Damas. The other is his younger brother, Sir Ontzlake. Their father died and left all he had to the sons. Sir Damas and Sir Ontzlake were to share the money and castles. Little by little Sir Damas took away what his brother had. Sir Ontzlake now has but one castle left. Sir Damas is trying to get that away from him. He cannot get it by fighting Sir Ontzlake for it. Sir Ontzlake is a good knight and a strong fighter. Damas is afraid of him. But you know what the law says. If two knights fight, the winner is right. Sir Damas is trying to find a knight who will fight his brother for him. When he can catch a knight through his tricks, he brings him here. The knight must fight for Sir Damas or stay locked up here."

"And none of you men will do it?"

"No. We are true knights and will not fight for Sir Damas."

As they spoke, the door opened. In came a girl. She walked up to King Arthur.

"Sir," she said, "the lord of this castle sent me. If you will do battle for him, you may go free."

"Lady," said King Arthur, "I do not want to do battle for him. But tell him I will. If I win he must let all these men go free also."

"He will do so," said the girl. "I go to tell him."

"Wait!" cried Arthur. "I have seen your face before. Were you not on the boat last night?"

"I know nothing of a boat, sir," she said.

"I think you do," cried Arthur. "Have I not seen you at Camelot? Have you not

49

been with Queen Morgan le Fay there?"

"No, my lord. I have never seen Queen Morgan le Fay. I am Sir Damas' daughter."

"Well," said Arthur, "go tell your father I must send a letter home. If I fight, I must have my own sword."

"He will send the letter," said the girl.

So King Arthur wrote to Queen Morgan, telling her to send Excalibur. The Queen, whose plans were working well, smiled at the letter. "He shall have a sword," she said. "And he will think he has Excalibur." So the Queen sent the false Excalibur which she had had made. She herself carefully wrapped Excalibur and hurried from the castle.

During this time Sir Damas sent word to Sir Ontzlake. "I have a knight to do battle with you," he wrote. "I say that your castle and lands rightly belong to me. If my knight beats you, you must give them up."

Now Sir Ontzlake did not know what to do. A few days before, he had been hurt in battle. Both his legs were badly cut and he could not leave his bed. He had no friend near to battle for him. As he read his brother's letter, a boy came in to say a lady wished to see him.

"Bring her here," said Sir Ontzlake.

The lady was a stranger to him, but looked as if she were a queen.

"Sir Ontzlake," she said, "I have heard of your trouble. I can get a brave knight to do battle for you."

"How do you know all this, lady?" cried Sir Ontzlake.

"I know many things," smiled the lady. "Come. You cannot fight. Your brother Sir Damas has a strong knight on his side. I will bring you a better one."

"Who is he?" asked Sir Ontzlake.

"Sir Accalon of the Round Table of King Arthur."

"He is a good knight and a mighty fighter. As I cannot ride, I will be glad to have him."

"Have no fear," said the lady. "He will be ready."

Later that day another lady stood looking down at a sleeping knight. He woke to find himself beside a pool in a forest.

"Where am I?" he cried. "And where is my lord, King Arthur?" He looked up and saw the lady standing nearby.

"Welcome, Sir Accalon," said the lady. "I need your help."

"Lady, I am a knight of the Round Table. We are always ready to help those who need us. What can I do?"

"There lives near here a good knight, Sir Ontzlake. His brother, Sir Damas, is trying to take his land and castle from him. Sir Damas has a knight to fight for him. Sir Ontzlake is wounded. He has no one to fight for him."

"Lady," said Sir Accalon, "I would be glad to fight for Sir Ontzlake. But I have no armor nor sword."

"Sir Ontzlake will gladly give you armor. I have a sword for you. Wait."

She went off and soon came back with a sword. Sir Accalon could hardly believe his eyes. The sword was Excalibur!

"This sword is yours if you will fight," said the lady.

"I know that sword," said Sir Accalon.

"I have heard there is another like it," said the lady.

"Lady, I will do anything to win this sword."

Sir Accalon went with her to Sir Ontzlake's castle. There he got armor and horse. The lady left soon after.

News of the battle soon went far and wide. People came from far and near to watch. King Arthur came in Sir Damas' armor, Sir Accalon in Sir Ontzlake's. Both had their helmets on and did not know each other.

A boy blew his horn to start the battle. The two bold knights rushed at each other. They crashed together and both spears flew into pieces. Arthur and Accalon jumped quickly from their horses. Now they ran together with their swords swinging. As they began to strike, Vivien came near the field. She stood to watch, not knowing which knight was King Arthur.

King Arthur struck again and again at Sir Accalon. But hard though his blows were, they flew off the other's armor. Sir Accalon struck, too, with Excalibur. Time after time the wonderful sword bit through Arthur's armor. Blood began to drip from the cuts. King Arthur knew something must be wrong. "Has my end come?" he thought. "Has my sword lost its magic? It seems as if my enemy must have both Excalibur and the magic cover!"

Arthur would not give up. Again he struck a hard blow. His sword hit Sir Accalon's helmet and he fell to his knees. As he did, Arthur's sword blade broke off. He stood holding the handle.

Accalon got up and struck Arthur a mighty blow. Now Arthur fell to his hands and knees.

Vivien had been watching the fight carefully. "That must be King Arthur who is down," she said to herself. She clapped her hands together as Merlin had taught her. Sir Accalon fell back. Excalibur dropped to the ground. Arthur reached blindly for it. He got it in his hands. Holding it high over his head he brought it down on the other's head. He hit him again, then again. Sir Accalon fell down. King Arthur knew now how he had been tricked. He pulled the sword cover away from Accalon's belt. He threw it away. Now Arthur pulled off Accalon's helmet, crying, "Who are you who has stolen my sword?"

"I am King Arthur's true knight, Sir Accalon! I stole no sword!"

"Sir Accalon? Do you not know your king?" He took off his own helmet. Sir Accalon fell back and lay still.

The people now saw that their king was there. They ran forward to help him off the field. Vivien ran forward.

"He is badly hurt," she cried. "I can help heal him."

They carried both Arthur and Accalon away to a castle near by. Vivien put Merlin's magic medicine on Arthur's wounds. So wonderful was this medicine that Arthur's wounds healed in a day.

Arthur now asked Sir Accalon what had

happened to him. He soon saw that somebody had tricked him but that it was not Sir Accalon.

Now King Arthur called Sir Damas and Sir Ontzlake to him.

"Sir Damas," he said, "you are a bad knight. I take away all you have but one castle. All the rest goes to Sir Ontzlake. You may never again ride or fight as a knight. You must free all those men in your castle. Go your way."

News soon came to Queen Morgan le Fay that her plan had failed. "Does my brother know what I did?" she asked herself. "I must find out." So she set out for Camelot again.

When she got to the castle, she boldly went to see the king.

"Where is my lord, King Arthur?" she asked.

"He has just come back. He sleeps. We may not wake him."

"I will go in to him," she said.

She slipped softly into the room. King Arthur lay sound asleep.

"I will steal Excalibur again," she thought. "This time he shall never get it back."

But then she saw that Arthur held the sword in his hand as he slept. She did not dare try to take it. The sword cover lay on the bed. Queen Morgan took it and slipped out. In a few minutes she was riding as fast as she could go.

When King Arthur awoke, he saw the magic cover was gone.

"Who has been in this room?" he cried.

"Queen Morgan le Fay," said his men.

"Morgan again!" cried Arthur. "Come! After her!"

Morgan le Fay saw them coming. She beat her horse and raced on. Soon she came past a lake. She took the cover and threw it with all her might.

Just as it was about to fall into the water, a strange thing happened. A woman's arm came out of the lake. The cover fell into the hand. Slowly the arm and cover went down. Never again did any man see the magic cover of Excalibur.

King Arthur and his men had seen what had happened. King Arthur stopped his horse.

"We can catch her," cried the men.

Arthur shook his head sadly. "Let her go," he said. "The cover is gone. It will do no good to harm her. She is an evil woman."

So the magic cover was lost. A day was to come when King Arthur needed that cover badly. That you shall read about later.

The Kitchen Knight

Once a year King Arthur and his Round Table had a great feast. King Arthur loved adventure. As he was king, he could no longer go himself on many adventures. He often sent his knights of the Round Table to help those in need. When a strong knight harmed his people, they often came for help. Then he might send his greatest knight, Sir Lancelot of the Lake. He often sent the bold Sir Gawain. Gawain was Lancelot's friend and the son of King Lot. King Lot had married Arthur's sister Margaret. Gawain and Sir Gaheris, Gawain's brother, had long been in King Arthur's court. They had made their home with their uncle, King Arthur. King Arthur loved Gawain above all except Lancelot.

Now at this great feast Arthur would not eat until he had sent someone on an adventure or he had given someone help. As he sat down, a tall, handsome young man came in. Everyone looked at his hands. They were very large and white and strong. When he came to the table they saw he was a foot taller than most men.

"My lord king," said the young man, "I ask three gifts. One I ask for now, the others I will ask in one year."

"Ask," said King Arthur. "You shall have your wish."

"The first is that you let me live in your kitchen for a year."

"That is easy. Who are you? You look as if you come from a good family."

"I may not tell my name, if you please."

"Do as you will. Sir Kay, here is a man for kitchen work. Treat him kindly and give him what he needs."

"He doesn't need much," said Sir Kay.

"If he were worth anything he would ask for armor and sword. If he has no name I'll give him one. See those pretty hands! I'll call him Pretty Hands. He can live in the kitchen like a pig."

"You need not be so sour," said Sir Lancelot. "He looks like a good strong lad."

"Yes," said Sir Gawain, "he may make a good knight."

"He is just a lazy fellow," said Sir Kay.

So Pretty Hands went to the kitchen. Later Sir Lancelot and Sir Gawain told him they would help him if he wished. The lad would take no help. "I will obey Sir Kay and work in the kitchen," he said.

He did everything he was told and did it cheerfully. Whenever the knights fought, he was there to watch. In the matches among the young men, he always won, for he was strong and quick. When Sir Kay made fun of him, he never got angry.

A year passed. Again it was time for the feast. Again King Arthur would not begin to eat. Then a young woman came into the hall. She kneeled before King Arthur.

"King Arthur, I come for help!" she cried.

"What help do you need?" asked the king.

"My lord, I am called Linet. My sister, the beautiful Lady Lyon, cannot leave her castle. A cruel knight will not let her leave unless she will marry him. Please send a knight of your famous Round Table to save her."

"Who is this false knight?" asked Arthur.

"Sir, he is known far and wide as the Red Knight."

"I have heard of him," said Sir Gawain. "Uncle, he is a mighty fighter. He has killed some of our knights."

Out of the kitchen came Pretty Hands. He ran to the king.

"My lord," he cried, "a year has gone by. Now I ask my second gift."

As he came near the girl, she held her nose and looked away.

"Speak," said King Arthur.

"Send me on this adventure."

"I will keep my word," said Arthur. "You may go."

"My lord, this is my third gift. Send Sir Lancelot to follow me. When I prove myself, he shall make me a knight."

"If he wishes, Sir Lancelot may go."

The girl stamped her foot angrily. "Shame!" she cried. "I ask for a knight and I get a kitchen boy!" She ran from the hall and jumped on her horse.

King Arthur sent for armor and a horse for Pretty Hands. When he put on the armor, the knights all looked twice. He was taller than ever and rode his horse well.

While Pretty Hands got ready, Sir Kay watched angrily. When he had ridden off after the girl, Sir Kay jumped up.

"That kitchen boy in armor!" he cried. "I'll see if he still knows I am his master."

Lancelot laughed. "You had better be careful, Sir Kay," he said. "He is a big boy now."

Sir Kay rode off after the boy.

He caught up with him just as Pretty Hands rode up to Linet.

"Turn around, Pretty Hands," called Sir Kay. "Do you not know me?"

"Yes," said the boy quietly. "I know you. You are the worst of all the Round Table. Do not come near me."

"You need a lesson!" cried Sir Kay. He pointed his spear and rode hard at the boy. Pretty Hands had only his sword, for he had taken no shield or spear. As Sir Kay's spear was about to strike him, he cleverly slapped it aside with his sword. He swung the sword back easily in his big hand and knocked Sir Kay to the ground. Then he jumped from his horse. Calmly he took Sir Kay's shield and spear. Sir Kay jumped on his horse and rode for home.

As he did, Sir Lancelot, who had followed, rode up. He laughed so hard he could hardly stay on his horse.

"Good boy!" he cried. "That was well done."

"Sir," said the boy, "will you make me a knight now? I would rather have you do it than any knight in the world."

"I will," said Sir Lancelot. "But I must

know your name and your father's name."

"Sir, my name is Gareth. I am the son of King Lot and Queen Margaret."

"What!" cried Sir Lancelot. "The brother of Sir Gawain and Sir Gaheris? But they did not know you!"

"They left home when I was very young. I begged to follow them to King Arthur's court. My queen mother did not want me to go. At last she said I could if I would not fight for a full year. I gave her my word. That is why I lived in the kitchen."

Sir Lancelot gladly made him knight. Pretty Hands became Sir Gareth.

Then Gareth rode after Linet again. When he caught up with her, she pulled her horse aside.

"What do you want?" she cried. "Get away! You smell of the kitchen, you kitchen boy. I don't want you to ride near me."

"Lady Linet," said Gareth gently, "I was a kitchen boy. But I have a strong arm to help you. Did you not see me knock Sir Kay down?"

"It was a trick! You are a coward!

Pretty Hands! Go home and wash the dishes, Pretty Hands."

Gareth would not get angry. "Say what you will," he said. "I will not leave. I told King Arthur I would save your sister, Lady Lyon. I will do it or I will die trying."

"You kitchen fool! Ride on, then. You won't last long."

They rode on together then. As they came through a dark forest, a boy came running to them.

"My lord knight!" he called. "Ride away fast. Six robbers have just taken my master."

"Where are they?" asked Gareth. The boy pointed to some trees. Gareth turned his horse and rode toward them. Three men jumped from the bushes. They swung great clubs and called Gareth to stop.

Gareth swung his sword right and left, dropping two dead. The third got the flashing blade in his back as he ran away. The other three dropped their clubs and ran for their lives. Gareth found the knight tied to a tree. Gareth got him loose.

"Thank you," he cried to Gareth. "They were about to kill me. You and your lady must stop at my castle. I must pay you for saving my life."

"I will take nothing," said Gareth. "I cannot take gold for doing my duty. If the lady wishes, we will stay with you tonight."

As it was getting dark, Linet agreed to stay at the castle. When food was brought, she would not eat with Gareth.

"Get him away," she said. "He is King Arthur's kitchen boy. I am a lady. He is not fit to eat with me."

"Lady," said the knight, "what do you mean? This man is a knight. Did you not see him save me from the robbers?"

"They were cowards. He is no fighter."

"Well," said the knight, "he's good enough for me. I will eat with him and you can sit alone if you wish."

So Linet ate alone while Gareth and the knight talked and laughed over their dinner. Next morning Linet and Gareth again started out.

They soon came to a stream. On the

other side two knights sat waiting on their horses. They held their spears as if to keep them from crossing.

"Now, kitchen boy," laughed Linet, "what now? Here are two knights. You had better run back to your dishes."

Gareth rode into the water. One knight rode to meet him. Their spears broke as they crashed in the middle of the stream. They jumped into the water and began to fight with swords.

Gareth struck only once. The mighty blow knocked the knight flat. The rushing water carried him away.

Gareth now got back on his horse just in time. The second knight rode at him, his spear aimed at Gareth's heart. Again Gareth knocked the spear aside. Before the knight could ride past, Gareth's sword broke his helmet wide open. He, too, fell into the water. Gareth rode across to the other shore and waited for Linet.

"Lucky!" she cried, as her horse climbed the bank. "How a kitchen boy could beat two knights, I don't know. The first knight's horse fell. You hit the second when he wasn't looking. You can't fight fair."

"Lady Linet," said Gareth, "say what you will. I am a true knight and I do fight fair. Someday I will win kind words from you."

"Never!" cried Linet.

Again they went on their way. Late in the afternoon they came to a forest. A long black spear stood in their path. A big black war horse was tied to a tree. On a stone nearby sat a knight in black armor.

"Run, dish washer," said Linet. "That is the Black Knight. He will kill you if you try to pass."

"Lady," called the Black Knight, "is that a knight from King Arthur's court? Is he your champion?"

"Ha!" laughed Linet. "He is no knight. He just follows me."

"Then he will have to give me his horse, armor, and sword," said the Black Knight.

"Why don't you try to take them?" said Gareth.

Angrily the Black Knight rode at Gareth. Gareth's spear held true and the Black Knight was badly wounded. He pulled out his sword and fought hard. Soon he grew weaker. At last he fell from his horse.

Gareth now took the knight's black armor and put it on. He rode on after Linet. Again she scolded him and told him he had not fought fair. Again Gareth spoke only kind words to her.

In the forest they soon met another knight in their path. This one wore green armor.

"Is that you, my brother?" he called.

"No," said Linet. "He is not your brother, the Black Knight. He is King Arthur's kitchen boy. He just killed your brother and took his armor."

"Then he shall die!" cried the Green Knight. He rushed down the path at Gareth. Again Gareth's spear struck through the other's armor. Horse and man were thrown to the ground. The Green Knight got to his feet and ran at Gareth. Gareth jumped down to give him a fair chance.

The Green Knight was stronger than his brother and was a better fighter. Again and again he struck Gareth.

"Can you not beat a kitchen boy?" called Linet.

The Green Knight angrily swung a mighty blow. Gareth caught it on his shield, but the shield split apart. Before he could pull back his sword, Gareth drove him to his knees.

In a flash he had pulled off the Green Knight's helmet. He held him by the hair and raised his sword.

"Spare me!" cried the Green Knight.

"I will cut off your head unless the Lady Linet asks me to spare you," said Gareth.

"I'll not beg you for anything!" cried Linet.

"Then off comes his head," said Gareth.

"Lady," cried the Green Knight, "say a kind word for me! Sir, spare me! I have many knights under me. We will all serve you if I live."

"You coward!" said Linet. "Will you give up to a dish washer?"

Gareth raised his sword and started to swing.

"Stop!" cried Linet. "Do not kill him!"

Gareth smiled. "Since you ask it, I will spare him," he said.

Gareth told him to take his knights to Camelot. "Tell the King that I beat you fairly," he said. They stayed that night at the Green Knight's castle. Linet was angrier than ever because she had had to ask Gareth a favor. In the morning they set out once more for the Lady Lyon's castle.

Soon they came near a city. "Now you will meet your match," said Linet. "The great knight Sir Persant lives there. He has never been beaten. Turn around and go back while you have a chance. He has many knights who serve him."

Gareth laughed. "I will be glad to meet him," he said. "I hope you soon learn that I fear no man. I said I would fight to free your sister. Nothing can stop me."

At last Linet's heart grew softer. "My lord," she said, "I know you have fought well. You must be tired. Do go back. I do not want you killed. This Sir Persant is a famous fighter. Even if you beat him, you must face the Red Knight. The Red Knight is strong as seven good knights. I think no knight but Sir Lancelot can overcome him."

"I must. It is my duty," said Gareth.

"Will you forgive my bad words?"

"I will."

As they talked a knight came riding swiftly toward them.

"It is Sir Persant himself," cried Linet. "Get ready!"

Gareth rode forward to meet him. Their horses crashed together. Their spears flew into pieces. Sir Persant was upon Gareth like a tiger. Gareth had learned much in his other fights. Calmly he met Sir Persant's rushes. As the other grew weaker, Gareth fought harder. For more than an hour they fought, breaking and cutting the armor.

Sir Persant made a last rush to overcome Gareth. The boy was ready. He smashed Sir Persant's helmet a terrible blow. Down he went, flat on his face. Gareth put his foot on the other Knight's back and jerked his helmet loose. Linet ran up and held Gareth's sword arm.

"Save his life, my lord," she said. "I pray you spare him."

"I will," said Gareth. "He is a good knight and has fought well."

"I am beaten fairly," said Sir Persant. "I give myself up and my men."

That night Gareth and Linet stayed at Sir Persant's castle. In the morning Sir Persant rode to the gate with them.

"You go to the Castle Dangerous," he said. "This is a hard adventure. The Red Knight is strong as seven men. He keeps Lady Lyon in the castle hoping that Sir Lancelot or King Arthur will try to save her. He hates all knights of the Round Table. More than others he hates Lancelot and Arthur. Good luck to you, young man. My men and I will ride to Camelot to tell Arthur what has happened."

They were now close to the Castle Dangerous of the Lady Lyon. As they rode on

they saw shields and armor hanging from the trees.

"Those belong to knights whom the Red Knight has killed," said Linet.

They came then to a tall tree. A great horn hung from a branch.

"If you want to fight the Red Knight, you must blow that horn," said Linet.

Gareth rode up to the horn and blew upon it. They could now see knights jump upon their horses. Far down the road stood a castle. Around the castle were hundreds of tents.

Gareth saw a tall, strong man run from a tent. A knight handed him his helmet. Another gave him spear, shield, and sword. The sun shone on his bright red armor. Sword, spear, and shield were also red. He rode out to the field before the castle. There he stopped his horse to wait for his enemy.

"That is the Red Knight," said Linet. "See, there in the large castle window sits Lady Lyon, my sister."

Gareth looked up. There he saw the

most beautiful lady he had ever seen. She smiled and waved to him.

"Do not look at her," called the Red Knight. "She is my lady and shall never be yours. Who are you, Black Knight? What is your name?"

"I am not ready to tell my name," said Gareth. "When I kill you I shall join the knights of the Round Table."

"Get ready!" cried the Red Knight.

He dug his spurs into his great horse and drove forward. Gareth rushed to meet him. Their spears flew into pieces and the saddles were torn from the horses. Both knights were thrown to the ground. They crawled to their feet and drew their swords.

Never were such mighty blows struck. Their armor began to break off and the shields bent and broke. Hour after hour they fought. The Red Knight was the greatest fighter young Gareth had ever met. They fought on until evening. They agreed to rest and tie up their worst wounds.

Gareth looked up at the castle window.

The Lady Lyon had not moved. She waved to him again.

"Are you ready?" cried Gareth.

The Red Knight put on his helmet again. The fight went on now hotter than ever. Then suddenly the Red Knight twisted Gareth's sword out of his hand. He hit Gareth hard and felled him. Then he ran forward and threw himself on him.

Gareth rolled over and jumped to his feet. He picked up his sword just in time. The Red Knight got to his feet and rushed. Gareth's sword met him coming in. One last mighty blow drove him to the ground. Gareth was upon him and tore his helmet loose.

"I give up!" screamed the Red Knight.

"Did you spare the ones you overthrew?" cried Gareth. "You are not fit to live." Down came Gareth's sword. The Red Knight fell back dead. A great shout rose from the castle.

Gareth spoke now to the Red Knight's men. "Go to King Arthur," he said. "Tell him his kitchen boy sent you."

A band of knights was seen toward the castle.

"They are Knights of the Round Table!" cried Gareth happily.

Sir Lancelot had taken the news to King Arthur that Pretty Hands was King Lot's son. Sir Gawain and Sir Gaheris were as surprised as anyone that the kitchen boy was their brother.

Soon afterward all went back to Camelot. The beautiful Lady Lyon and Sir Gareth were married. Lady Linet and Sir Gaheris were married at the same time. Lady Linet always had sharp words for everyone, but all knew she had a kind heart. Sir Gareth became a knight of Arthur's Round Table and did many brave deeds before his death.

Sir Galahad and the Holy Grail

Many years before, Merlin had told King Arthur many things which would happen. He had said that the Knights of the Round Table would become famous. When all 150 seats of the Round Table were filled, sad days would come. Arthur's enemies would come into England. Some of his knights would prove false. Old friends would become enemies. King Arthur himself would die in battle.

All happened as Merlin had said. Sir Lancelot of the Lake had come to Camelot. He had proved himself the greatest fighter of all. He had fought for Queen Guinevere in battle. Of all Knights of the

Round Table, Queen Guinevere loved Lancelot best.

Merlin had said that the Danger Seat of the Round Table could be filled by only one man. That man would be the greatest knight of all. He would do no wrong and be kind and gentle. This knight was to come four hundred fifty-four years after Jesus had died. This knight was to be the one to win the Holy Grail.

The old stories said that Jesus had a secret follower named Joseph. Before Jesus died, he had the Last Supper with his twelve closest followers. Together they had eaten and had drunk from one cup. After the supper Joseph had carried off this cup to keep it safe. The next day Jesus had been nailed to the cross.

The old stories told that Joseph had held the cup and caught Jesus' blood. When a Roman soldier wounded Jesus with a spear, Joseph begged for the spear. Joseph kept the cup and spear hidden away.

The Roman ruler threw Joseph into

prison for many years. At last he got free. He came then to England. There he built a castle and kept the spear and cup. The years went on. Joseph died, but his sons and sons' sons held the castle. The cup became known as the Holy Grail. Often it healed the sick and did other wonderful things. Few knew where the Holy Grail was kept.

In the days of Arthur, Sir Lancelot once came to this castle. He was able to free a lady from the magic tricks of Queen Morgan le Fay. Lancelot gave other help to the lord of the castle. He learned about the secret of the castle. Lancelot stayed long. A son was born to him and the Lady Elaine. They named the son Galahad. Merlin had known that Galahad was to fill the Seat of Danger at the Round Table.

There came news now to King Arthur that his people fought among themselves. They did not obey the laws of Arthur or of the church. Arthur asked help from the men of the church.

"Our country is in great danger," they told him. "The old stories tell us that three good knights shall help you. We pray that all men will do as they will do. If they do, our land will have peace. If they do not, we shall have trouble and war."

Soon after that a knight came to Arthur to join the Round Table. News of him had been coming to Camelot for a long time. The knights all saw that he was good and gentle. He fought those who did wrong and helped the weak. This Sir Percival became a Knight of the Round Table. King Arthur soon knew he was one of the three good knights.

There also came back to Camelot Sir Bors. Sir Bors was of Lancelot's family. He had long been away finding adventure. He had done great deeds and showed himself a true knight. "Sir Bors may well be the second of the three good knights," thought King Arthur.

The time came again for the feast of the Round Table. All the knights would come to Camelot to promise again to live as true knights. The knights had all come into the great hall. Each knight stood at his place.

Never before had a name been seen on the Danger Seat. Now they saw these words —

This seat shall be filled 454 years after our Lord died.

"Brothers," said Sir Lancelot, "this must be the very day. Four hundred fifty-four years have passed since Christ died."

They saw the names on the seats on both sides of the Seat of Danger. The right one had the name of Sir Percival. The left had the name of Sir Bors. All seats were filled but the Danger Seat. They began to eat and drink.

Suddenly the door opened. An old man came into the hall. His clothes were white. His long hair and beard were white. With the old man came a young knight in red armor. The old man led the young one up to King Arthur.

"My lord," he said, "I bring the last knight for your Round Table. He shall help fight the battle for our land. His name is Galahad."

"You are welcome," said King Arthur.

The old man led Galahad to the Danger Seat.

The knights all held their breath. Merlin had said this seat was for one man only. All others who dared sit there would be struck dead.

"This is your seat," said the old man. "You only can win the Holy Grail. Those whose hearts are clean will help you."

"What must my knights do to win the Holy Grail?" said King Arthur. "Will the Holy Grail bring us peace to end our war?"

"No man can tell you that," said the old man. "When your people did right, the Holy Grail stayed in our land. Now they fight among themselves. Now they do evil. They are proud. Unless they change, the Holy Grail shall leave our land. When it does, war and trouble will be upon us."

The old man left. Then Sir Gawain arose.

"I do not know what you others will do,"

he said. "But tomorrow I leave. I will go to find the Holy Grail. If I can find it, I will save our land."

Now others sprang to their feet. "I, too!" they cried. "And I."

The tears came to King Arthur's eyes. "Gawain, you are right. You must go. This is a sad day for me. All my Round Table will leave me. I fear we shall never meet again."

The next morning the knights got ready to leave. They put on armor and took swords, shields, and spears. All said good-bye to King Arthur and Queen Guinevere. The streets of Camelot were lined with people. Rich and poor were out to see the famous knights leave. Two by two these mighty heroes rode out into the world.

"How many will come back?" said Queen Guinevere. She wiped her eyes.

"I fear not many," said King Arthur sadly.

Sir Galahad rode to the north. As he rode he grew sad to see how men lived. He tried to make peace among those who fought. "Our enemies are coming against us," he told them. "Let us not fight among ourselves." Some listened and went to join Sir Bedevere to fight the enemy. Others would not go. Farmers would not work in the fields, for robbers stole the crops. Weeds grew everywhere. The lords locked their doors and let no stranger in. Bad times had come to Arthur's land.

One morning Sir Galahad saw a band of strange men riding toward the sea. He saw they were leading a knight to the high cliffs. His armor was broken and bloody. Galahad saw they meant to throw him from the cliff.

From a forest now came a lone knight riding to meet them. The knight wore white armor. On his white shield was a blood red heart. Sir Galahad rode to meet him, for he knew that shield. Only Sir Percival carried a white shield with a red heart.

"Stop!" cried Sir Percival to the men.

"Who are you?" called the men, getting their swords ready.

"A Knight of King Arthur's Round Table. You have there my true friend, Sir Bors!"

"Come and get him! King Arthur is no king of ours. We rule ourselves." Seven knights broke loose and rode against Sir Percival.

All at once Sir Galahad's horse flew at the band. He was upon them before they knew it. He threw three down before his spear broke. Then he took his sword and drove the others from Sir Bors. Seeing his chance, Sir Bors pulled a sword from an enemy's hand.

Bors and Galahad now turned to help Sir Percival. Percival had already cut down his enemies. The three soon sent the band of strangers flying.

They looked happily at one another. "Let us go on together," said Galahad. "Let us fight together until death parts us."

Slowly they moved to the north, fighting wrong and trying to make peace. At last they came to an old castle. At the castle windows were wild, strange men. They had long yellow hair and wore helmets with great horns.

"They are the enemy from across the sea," said Galahad. "They have taken this castle from the owner. They have come to win our land and kill our king."

The men in the castle had seen them. The gate dropped. Ten knights came riding out. Behind them rushed the wild strangers on foot.

"The knights are our own people," cried Sir Bors. "They are fighting for the enemy! Down with them!"

The three brave knights charged forward together. They made a quick end of the false knights. Galahad and Percival fought them with spear and sword. Sir Bors rode like a devil among the footmen. The swords flashed like lightning, cutting down the enemy. When the wild strangers saw their knights were down, they ran for the castle.

Galahad, Percival, and Bors were close upon them. Before the castle gate could close, the three war horses thundered over the bridge. The strangers now ran into the castle itself, to their friends. Again the three knights did not stop.

Their swords dripped blood as they stormed through the castle. Never were so many killed by so few. From hall to room they ran, killing all before them. At last they were so tired they had to rest. First they freed those who had been in the castle.

Among these was an old man. He told the others to clean the castle, and throw out the dead. "You are great knights," said the old man. "You have saved the holy things in this castle. I know you are the three who were to do this. Now you shall see a wonderful thing."

He took the three to a room and left them alone. Suddenly the doors and windows closed. The wind began to blow. The room grew dark. Then from above came a bright stream of light. In the light they saw a table. On the table stood a shining silver cup. Near it they could see a spear

with blood dripping from the point of it.

Then they saw the face of an old man.

"I am Joseph," he said softly. "I am the Joseph who took our Lord's body from the cross."

Galahad, Percival, and Bors looked at one another. This man had been dead for over four hundred years!

"Do not be afraid," he said. "I am not a living man of your world. I will do you no harm."

He took the shining silver cup and moved close to Galahad. He took food from it and gave it to him. Then he gave to Percival and Bors.

"Do you know this cup?" he said.

"I do not know it," said Galahad.

"It is the Holy Grail."

"We have tried to find it two years."

"None other in this land shall see it. Tonight it goes from this land."

"Then our country shall fall!" cried Galahad.

"Yes. It is now an evil land. I brought the Grail here four hundred fifty winters ago. Now I take it away. You three have fought bravely, but you could not change the evil ones. You three have tried to find the Holy Grail. Galahad and Percival, you have done no evil. Your work on earth is done. I will take you with me. Sir Bors, you still want to fight on. You are to stay to fight for your Lord longer."

The light grew brighter. Sir Bors threw his arm before his eyes. When he could see again, Joseph and the table were gone. Sir Galahad's and Sir Percival's arms were raised. They looked like men of stone. Sir Bors looked closely and saw they were dead.

Sir Bors buried them in the castle. Then he rode south toward Camelot.

He told King Arthur and what knights there were left what had happened. All knew then that Sir Galahad and Sir Percival had won the Holy Grail.

Sir Bors said nothing about the evil days which were to come.

Sir Lancelot Saves the Queen

One by one the knights who had tried to win the Holy Grail came back. Many had been killed, but King Arthur did not lose them all. Queen Guinevere was glad that Sir Lancelot and Sir Bors were safe. Lancelot had always fought for her. Sir Bors was Lancelot's cousin and good friend.

There were now evil men even at Arthur's court. One of the worst was Sir Modred. Modred was a brother of Gawain, Gareth, and Gaheris. Modred was jealous of Lancelot and Bors. He told lies about Lancelot and Queen Guinevere to the other knights. When Gawain heard these lies he almost killed his own brother Modred. Gawain loved Lancelot above all men. There were few who liked Modred.

The evil stories did not stop. Some said that Sir Lancelot had grown proud. Some said he planned to kill Arthur, take Guinevere as queen, and rule as king. Lancelot was fighting in the north for King Arthur and knew nothing about this.

Modred was too sly to tell these lies himself. He got Sir Pinel, another false knight, to do it. Men soon saw that Queen Guinevere was cold and angry when Sir Pinel was near.

At last Guinevere could keep still no longer. She planned a great dinner for the knights. There she would tell them about the lies. She would ask them to help her. To the dinner came the twenty-four knights who were left at the Round Table. Gawain and his brothers came, as did Modred and Pinel. Pinel's cousin, Sir Mador, came also.

The Queen and others knew that Gawain loved a certain kind of apple. For the dinner she had the kind of apples which Gawain liked. Sly Modred knew this, too. To get even with Gawain, Modred stole all the apples but one. Then he put a deadly poison into this apple. He knew the knights would leave this apple for Gawain.

After the dinner, the fruit was put on the table. Sir Pinel saw there was but one apple, which Gawain would want. As he, too, hated Gawain, he took the apple himself. He bit into it. His face grew white. "I am poisoned!" he cried. He fell to the floor screaming and kicking. Suddenly he lay still. Sir Pinel was dead.

The knights looked at one another, then at Guinevere. The same thought came to each one. Guinevere had heard the lies and had poisoned Pinel! None would look at her. One by one they started to leave the room.

"Stop!" cried Sir Mador. He held up the apple. "Look! This has killed my cousin, Sir Pinel." He turned to the Queen. "You killed him!" he cried. "I say you killed him! Queen or not, you must pay."

No one would speak for the Queen.

"I did not!" cried Guinevere. "I know nothing about it!" As she spoke she fell fainting to the floor. Modred smiled and said nothing.

The next day Sir Mador came before the King and charged Guinevere with murder.

"My queen has not done this, I know," said Arthur. "I am judge in this case. Our law says I may not fight to defend her. I know one of my knights will."

"If no knight will defend her, she must be burned at the stake," said Sir Mador. "So says the law. The Queen is not above the law. Name the day of battle, my lord."

"My lord," said Gawain, "none at the dinner may defend the Queen. Men will say such a knight helped the Queen and is against you."

"I must set the date if I am to be fair," said Arthur. "Sir Mador, be ready to fight the Queen's defender in fifteen days. If no one defends her, she must die by fire."

The Queen was now locked in her rooms. Knights were sent to guard the door. Guinevere sent for Sir Bors.

"I did not do it," she cried. "Sir Bors, will you not defend me? Lancelot is gone. I am without friends."

"I cannot do it," said Sir Bors. "I was at the dinner myself. But I will try to find Lancelot in time."

"Hurry! Hurry!" cried Guinevere. "Find him!"

Sir Bors rode from Camelot and sent men on different roads. Day and night he rode, hardly stopping. On the twelfth day he found Lancelot, badly wounded. Bors told him what had happened.

"They say the Queen did it?" cried Lancelot. "No one defends her? Then I will. Get my horse!"

He tied up his wounds and put on his armor. He and Sir Bors set out for Camelot. They did not stop for food and slept in their armor.

Lancelot was so angry he would not speak. In three days they were home. Sir

Bors went to tell the Queen Lancelot had come while Lancelot took off his armor.

The evil Modred was watching. While Bors was gone he told his friends more lies. "Sir Bors is helping Lancelot," he said. "He, too, wishes to kill King Arthur." Modred now set his friends to guard the Queen. When Bors went to see the Queen, they listened at the door. They quickly ran to Modred.

"Lancelot is back! He goes to see the Queen."

"Let him in," said Modred. "He will not have sword or armor. We will catch him there. Then we will bring him before the King."

So when Lancelot came, they let him in. The Queen told Lancelot her story.

"I will defend you tomorrow," he said. "You need not fear. I have always been your true knight."

Suddenly they heard shouts outside the door.

"False knight, Sir Lancelot! We have caught you! Come out, false Lancelot!"

Lancelot quickly guessed Modred's plan. He ran to the door and locked it.

"Is there armor here?" he asked.

"None," said the Queen. "Now they will kill you. You cannot fight them alone."

"They do not have me yet," said Lancelot. "Quiet!" he shouted. "I will open the door."

Lancelot unlocked the door. Then he held it open a bit. The first knight burst in. Quickly Lancelot slammed and locked the door. Before the knight knew what was happening, Lancelot had his sword. One swift blow and the knight lay senseless.

The men outside began to beat down the door. Lancelot put on the knight's armor. He unlocked the door and swung it open. One jump and he was in the narrow hall. Here only two men could face him at once.

Modred stayed back and called to the men to kill Lancelot. No two men could stand before the mighty Lancelot. In a few minutes seven men lay dead. Two lay wounded. Modred ran off screaming with

a deep cut in his arm. Lancelot went back to the Queen.

"I have killed some of Arthur's men," he said. "The King and Gawain will be against me now. Do not be afraid. I will save you."

Lancelot went to Sir Bors' room to rest. Sir Bors found out that Modred had run to King Arthur. Modred had told the King that Lancelot wanted his crown. Sir Bors now got Lancelot's friends together. He led them out to the forest. Here they met Lancelot to make their plans.

"My friends," said Lancelot, "you have heard these lies about me. I hold Arthur to be my king. But the Queen did no wrong. I cannot let her die."

"We will fight for you," cried Sir Bors.

"Yes! Yes!" shouted the knights.

"Then we will stay here. One will go to find out what Modred will do. We will save the Queen even if it means war."

Sir Mador went to the King.

"Lord," he said, "you must bring the Queen to the fire."

"I have given my word," said Arthur. "I will do it."

"And you must get Sir Lancelot," said Sir Modred. "He has killed our knights. Lancelot must die."

"Uncle," cried Gawain, "don't listen to him. Lancelot had to kill them. These are lies! Modred is my brother, but he is a liar!"

"He has always been a false knight!" said Gareth. "If you fight Lancelot, many friends will join him. We shall have war in our land."

"Lancelot has been a true knight," said Arthur. "I know he will defend the Queen. Let us send for him. He will answer you, Sir Modred."

So the King sent a man to bring Lancelot to Arthur. But Modred sent another to stop him. Modred's friend killed the King's man. Then he came running to King Arthur.

"I have just seen Lancelot and his friends," he cried. "When your man came near, Lancelot killed him. I heard him say that he feels you are his king no longer."

The King hung his head sadly. "I would not have believed it," he said. "Gawain, I have been too kind. Lancelot is mad. The Queen goes to the fire. Then we will catch Lancelot. Lancelot must die! Modred is right."

"You are wrong," said Gawain. "Lancelot has done no wrong."

Arthur sent Gareth and Gaheris to get the Queen. They had to lead her outside the city walls. Along the way the people cried and prayed. The knights rode after her. They went out to the wide fighting field. A wooden stake was driven into the ground. The men tied Guinevere to the pole. Then they piled wood around her. The Queen's face was white, but she said nothing. Women screamed and men's eyes held tears.

Modred's friends now gathered around the Queen. Sir Mador sat on his horse nearby. He was ready to fight if a defender should come.

Now a judge stepped forward. He said:

"Let all hear! So says King Arthur: The Queen has killed a knight by poison. His family ask her death. If any knight will defend her, let him come forward. If no knight defends her, she shall die by fire."

No one moved to help the Queen. Sir Modred smiled. The people looked down the road to the forest.

"Give the signal!" cried Sir Mador. "Sir Gaheris, obey the law!"

Sir Gaheris slowly raised his hand. A man ran with a burning branch to the Queen. He held it to the wood. The flames burst high.

Then came a noise like thunder. Down the road came a band of knights. A mighty knight led them. Everybody knew that shield!

"Sir Lancelot! Sir Lancelot!" shouted the people. "Save the Queen!"

With a crash they rode into Modred's men. Lancelot rode like a madman. His great sword cut down all who stood between him and the Queen. Before Gareth and Gaheris could move away, his great sword struck them down. Sir Mador's head was cut from his shoulders.

Modred's men broke and ran. Lancelot rode through the fire. He tore off the ropes which held the Queen. His great arm swung her to the saddle. Shouting to his men, Lancelot rode north to his own castle. Here he meant to guard her until she could safely go back to Arthur.

This was not to be. When Sir Gawain found his brothers dead, hate filled his eyes.

"I will not rest until I kill him!" he cried.

The last hope for peace was gone. King Arthur's land was torn with bitter war.

Death of King Arthur

Sir Gawain would not rest until he had killed Sir Lancelot. King Arthur and Gawain got their men and marched to Sir Lancelot's castle. Day after day they stormed the walls. The castle held fast. Lancelot did not want to fight King Arthur and tried to make peace. King Arthur was willing but Sir Gawain would not listen. Gawain had so many men that Arthur had to give in.

Once more Lancelot tried to make peace. He brought Queen Guinevere back to Arthur. The church leaders asked Arthur to take her back. Still Gawain would not agree to have Lancelot back at Camelot. Since

Lancelot owned castle and lands in France, he and his friends left.

The enemies of England began to make war on Arthur. Ship after ship landed on his shores. They killed and robbed the people. Then Arthur got together a great army. He fought many battles and drove the enemy off.

When Arthur was free from the enemy, Gawain wanted to fight Lancelot again. For a long time Arthur would not agree. At last he gave in. Arthur and Gawain fitted out ships and sailed. While Arthur was gone, Modred was to act as king.

When they landed on Lancelot's shores, Gawain's men burned down the houses. Lancelot's men begged him to fight Arthur and Gawain. But Lancelot was still true to Arthur.

"I will send a letter to King Arthur," he said. "He is my king. Maybe he will listen to me."

When Gawain saw the man with Lancelot's letter, he stopped him.

"Go!" he cried. "Tell Lancelot I will not

leave until I have fought him to the death."

Again Gawain and Arthur threw their army around Lancelot's castle. Gawain's men tried to break through but could not. Then Gawain rode alone to the castle.

"Where are you, false Lancelot?" he shouted. "Why do you hide, coward? Come out and fight me!"

"Lancelot," said Sir Bors, "you cannot hold back longer. Beat him down and end our troubles!"

"Yes," said Lancelot, "I must. He was long my dear friend. I never wanted to harm his brothers. Send my horse and bring my armor."

Lancelot rode out to meet Gawain. They rushed at each other like the wind. The horses fell and the spears broke. The swords began to fly.

When Gawain was a boy, Morgan le Fay had given him a magic power. Only King Arthur and Morgan knew the secret. This was the power: from morning until noon his strength grew greater. By noon he had the might of three men.

As they fought, Gawain grew stronger instead of weaker. Lancelot feared that some magic was working against him. He had fought many strong men before. So he did not rush Gawain but held back. He saved his own strength. Gawain rained blows on him again and again. He could not break Lancelot's guard. When the sun was straight above them, Gawain's blows grew lighter. Lancelot pressed forward now. He beat down Gawain's sword and shield. At last he hit his helmet a heavy blow. Gawain fell forward. Another blow and he went to the ground. Lancelot's friends watched to see him tear off the helmet and kill Gawain.

Lancelot put his sword into his belt and walked away.

"Why go?" cried Gawain. "Turn back and kill me! If you don't I will get you!"

"I will never kill you, Gawain," said Lancelot.

They carried Gawain back to his tent. He lay on his bed for weeks. When he could ride, he came to the castle gate again.

Once more Gawain called Lancelot to fight. Once more Lancelot rode to meet him. The fight went just as it had before. Gawain could not overcome Lancelot before noon. After that, Lancelot beat him to the ground. Gawain's old wound burst open.

Gawain was not to fight Lancelot again. Sir Bedevere came with bad news from home.

"Modred has risen against you," he cried. "He has formed an army to fight you. Guinevere is in prison."

King Arthur and Gawain now hurried back to fight Modred. Modred and his men were waiting. When King Arthur landed, a great army faced his men.

King Arthur led his men bravely into battle. Thousands of men on both sides were killed. Slowly Modred's men fell back. As Arthur rested after the last battle, a knight rode to him.

"My lord," he said, "Sir Gawain lies badly wounded. He cannot live long."

Sir Gawain lay in a boat near the shore.

"Uncle," he said, "I am done. I am hit

again where Sir Lancelot wounded me."

"Gawain!" cried Arthur. "Do not leave me. You are among the last of my brave knights."

"I have brought you evil," said Gawain. "There is no truer knight than Lancelot. He did not mean to kill my brothers. If only I could ask him to forgive me. I have brought on this war. Lift me, for I will write him a letter before I die."

So Gawain wrote and asked Lancelot to come help the King. When he finished he looked up at King Arthur.

"My lord," he said, "say you forgive me." As Arthur took him into his arms he died.

Arthur led his men against Modred. Slowly he pushed him back. At last they came near the lake where King Arthur had found Excalibur. The church leaders asked King Arthur to make peace.

"Our land is torn by war," they said. "Modred may give up. If you keep fighting, our best men will die. Let us ask him to meet you. Maybe he will listen."

Arthur agreed to meet Modred. They were to come halfway between the two armies. Each would bring the same number of men to the meeting.

"Have your spears ready," he told his men. "Modred is sly and full of tricks. If any man pulls his sword loose, charge them."

So they met. "You give me enough land," said Modred. "Agree that when you die I shall be king. If you do, we will stop fighting."

"I will give you nothing, Modred," said King Arthur. "I cannot trust you. You are a false knight."

Just then one of Modred's men felt a sting on his foot. He looked down and saw a snake had bitten him. He pulled out his sword to kill the snake.

Arthur's men were watching carefully. When they saw the sword flash, they cried out, "Charge!"

The two armies rushed together. Then there took place the longest and bloodiest battle of the war. King Arthur fought like a madman. The wonderful sword Excalibur struck down man after man. Thousands on both sides were killed that day.

At last King Arthur leaned on his sword. The dead lay all around him. Sir Lucan and Sir Bedevere stood at his side.

"Where are all my brave knights?" asked Arthur.

"Dead," said Bedevere. "Only we two are left of the Round Table."

"Where is that false Modred? I feel my end is near. He has done all this."

"Look," said Sir Lucan. He pointed to a knight standing alone. "There he stands."

"Give me my spear," said Arthur. Bedevere handed him a spear.

Modred saw him coming. He drew back his sword and took his shield. Arthur got under his shield with the spear. Through Modred's side it went. Modred knew his end had come. He threw himself forward on the spear. His last blow struck through Arthur's helmet and into his head. Modred dropped dead. Arthur fainted and fell upon him.

Bedevere and Lucan dragged Arthur to the nearby lake. They gave him water and washed his wound.

"Bedevere," said Arthur, "my end is near. Take my good sword Excalibur. Throw it far out into the lake. Then come back and tell me what you see."

Bedevere took the sword down to the lake. He saw no use in throwing the wonderful sword away. So he hid it and went back.

"What happened?" asked Arthur.

"Nothing," said Bedevere.

"Bedevere, you have lied to me. Will you not obey your king? Go, do as I told you."

So Bedevere took the sword and threw it far out into the lake. An arm reached out of the water and caught it. The arm shook the sword three times and was gone. Bedevere went back and told Arthur what had happened.

"Carry me to the lake," said Arthur.

When Bedevere got him there, he saw a flat black boat coming to shore. In it were women in black robes.

"Put me in the boat," said Arthur. Sir Bedevere watched the boat sail off with Arthur. He turned and walked away, not knowing where to go.

When morning came, he found a little church deep in the forest. He went in to pray. Inside he saw a great white stone box. On it were the words:

Here lies King Arthur

"I will stay here," said Bedevere. "I will watch and pray till I die. Then I will lie beside my king."

Sir Lancelot did not get Gawain's letter for many days. When he did, he hurried to help his king once more. First he went to where Gawain was buried.

"I was always ready to forgive you!" he cried. "Gawain, you were a brave and true knight."

Then the news of Arthur's battle came to him. The brave knights were all dead and King Arthur was gone. No man could say where.

"My friends," Lancelot said sadly, "we have come too late. Go back to your homes. I will look for King Arthur's body alone."

After many days Sir Lancelot came to the church. Here he found Sir Bedevere. Bedevere showed him where Arthur lay.

"I too shall spend my last days here," said Lancelot. And so he did.

Not long after, he heard that Guinevere, too, had died. He found her at last and brought her body back. He laid her gently beside King Arthur.

After that Lancelot would eat but little. Day after day he grew thinner and weaker. One morning Bedevere found him still and cold beside the stone box. A smile was on his face. Bedevere laid him at the feet of King Arthur and Queen Guinevere. On the stone above him Sir Bedevere cut these words:

Here lies Sir Lancelot of the Lake.
He was chief of King Arthur's knights.
He was a kind man, a true friend.
He did great deeds, but was gentle to the weak.
May he rest in peace.